WHAT HOLD HAS THIS MOUNTAIN

-Tao Hung Jing (452-536)

High up the mountain side
are more white clouds,
which I come to alone,
and cannot send you.

山 中 何 所 有

陶 弘 景 (梁 武 帝 時 代)

山 中 何 所 有 ，
嶺 上 白 雲 多 。
只 可 自 怡 悅 ，
不 堪 持 贈 君 。

IN FALL LEAVES

-Seng-Hsui-Mu (Monk in late
T'ang Dynasty, c.898-900)

Remembering the spring's sun,
believing the fall's wind.

落 葉 詩

　　　~ 僧 修 睦 （晚唐光化平間僧）

翻 思 向 春 日 ，

肯 信 有 秋 風 ？

Chinese Zen Poems

What Hold Has This Mountain?

san-tiong hô-so-iú

Translated by

Larry Smith
&
Mei Hui Huang

Bottom Dog Press
Laughing Buddha Series
Huron, Ohio

Cover Photo & Art by Mei Hui Huang
Front Cover Calligraphy by C. T. Huang
Title Page Calligraphy by Huang Chich-Ting

Laughing Buddha Series
Bottom Dog Press
c/o Firelands College
Huron, Ohio 44839

Table of Contents

8   Chinese Zen Poems: An Introduction

Pre-T'ang Dynasty

9   Return to the Idyllic Life of the Farmland -Tao Yuan Ming

10   Forewod to Body, Shadow, and Spirit -Tao Chien

11   I. The Body Speaks to the Shadow -Tao Chien

12   II. The Shadow Replies to the Body -Tao Chien

14   III. The Spirit Speaks -Tao Chien

16   Drinking -Tao Yuan Ming

17   Seng Chao's Death Poem - Seng Chao

18   Missing the Wild Geese - Ling Tsang

19   The Flower and Seen Sequence...

        I. Poem - Bodhidharma

        II. Poem - Hui-Ko

        III. Poem - Tseng Tsan

        IV. Poem - Tao Hsin

        V. Poem - Hung Jen

        VI. Poem - Hui-Neng

        VII. Poem -Huai-Jang

T'ang Dynasty

26   Poem of Enlightenment - Shen-Hsiu

27   Poem of Enlightenment - Hui-Neng

28   Flower Poem - Chih Hsuan

29   A Dream - Tao Kai

30   Leisure in the Autumn Night - Hsui Mu

31   Self-Portrait - Tan Chiao

32   A Foreword for Monk Chang's Portrait of a Drunken Monk - Huai-Su

33   From Cold Mountain Poems - Han Shan

37   Free Spirit - Shih Te

38   Poem Written on the Wall - Feng Kan

39   Song of Enlightenment - Hsuan Chyuen

40   Song of Sudden Enlightenment - Shen Hui

41   Poem from Old Pang - Pang Yun

42   Retiring to South Mountain at Year's End - Meng Hao-jan

43   Spring Dawn - Meng Hao-jen

44   Birds Sing in the Mountain Stream - Wang Wei

45   Hut Among the Bamboo - Wang Wei
46   Village of the Deer Stockade - Wang Wei
47   Wen-Apricot Hut - Wang Wei
48   Hibiscus Village - Wang Wei
49   A Poem - Wang Wei
50   From My Country Retreat By the River Wang
       After Heavy Rain - Wang Wei
52   In the Mountain - Wang Wei
53   My Retreat On South Mountain - Wang Wei
54   Night Thoughts - Li Po
55   Looking for Master Chang at South River - Liu
       Chang Ching
56   Response to Chang Yen's Poem—Autumn Night
       -Han Hung
57   Ch'in* - Yin Luan
58   On South Mountain - Tsu Yung
59   Moonlit Night - Liu Fang-Ping
60   Welcome - Tu Fu
61   Ascending - Tu Fu
62   A Flower Not a Flower - Pai-Chu-I
63   Reading a Poem on Yuan-Chiu in a Boat - Pai-Chu-I
64   River Snow - Liu-Tsung-Yuan
65   A Thought at Year's End - Wang Chien
66   This Human Life - Chiao Jan
67   Moon on Water - Chiao Jan
68   My Stay at a Mountain With a Moon - Chaio Jan
69   Sermon on Larger Self at Hu-An Province -Ciao Jan
70   Dedication for a Zen Monastery - Yu Fu
71   Anchored for the Night at Maple Bridge - Chang Chi
72   On Visiting a Hermit and Not Finding Him at Home
       - Wu Pen
73   A Poem for Duke Wang - Kuan Hsiu
74   Thinking of Master Chih-Ti - Kuan Hsiu
75   Poem (While Walking With the Emporoe) - Fa Yen
76   Poem - Fa Yen
77   Meeting an Older Man-Yin Luan
78   Diverting Myself - Kuei Jen

Sung Dynasty
79   A Sigh for Myself - Fa Yuan
80   Cold Night - Tu Hsiao Shan
81   Awakening from a Nap - T'sung Yeuh

82 In Praise of Chang Cha's "A Trip to the Mountain"
    -Hseuh Tou
83 An Allegory -Wang An Shih
84 Late Spring - Wang An Shih
85 Mount Lu Poems
    I. An Inscription Poem from the Wall of Hsi-Liu
    Temple - Su Shih
    II. Poem - Su Shih
    III. For the Master of Tung-Lin Temple - Su Shih
88 Mountain Journal - Chang Ling
89 Free from New Year's Greetings - Tao Kai
90 A Poem for Autumn - Kuo-Yin
91 Poem - Lin Chi Chung
92 Sailing a Small Boat on a Dam - Chu Hsi
93 A Comment on #1 - Chu Hsi
94 A Comment on Reading #2 - Chu Hsi
95 On Nan-Ch'uan's "Tao Is Ordinary Mind"
    - Wu-Men-Hui-Kai
96 To Master Y'ing - Yuan Hao-Wen

Yuan Dynasty

97   Autumn Thoughts - Ma Chih Yuan
98   Responding to Yung-Ming's Zen Rhymes
     - Wu Chien Hsien Tu
99   Living on a Mountain - Chin Kung
100 Chin Kung's Bequest Poem - Chin Kung

Ming Dynasty

101 Traveling South - Cheng Mien
102 On a Monk Mending His Clothes - Ta Tung
103 Mountain Poem - Han Shan Te Ching
104 Mountain Living - Han Shan Te Ching
105 Mountain Journal - Han Shan Te Ching

Ch'ing Dynasty

106 Reply to Mr. Lee, Alms Giver - Fo-E
107 This Busy Struggle - Shih Lien
118 Sitting in the Sun - Shu-Liang
109 To Master I-Chuan - Jsu-Yun
110 Writing My Feelings in Late Autumn - Ching An
111 An Old Sail - Chun An
112 Selected Sources

CHINESE ZEN POEMS: An Introduction

On one level this book is the work of a decade of translation carried on at a true Taoist pace. From soon after Mei Hui Huang came to Ohio from Taiwan and became my student, then friend and teacher, we began passing work back and forth. Now that she is back in Taiwan we have continued to pass poems, translations, versions, suggestions, and revisions across the mountains and rivers.

On another deeper level the work of this book extends for almost two thousand years to the very roots of Zen Buddhism in China. The poets and poems which we selected cover a wide range of subjects and times, yet all contain the clear essence of Zen. Like all Zen art, the poems refuse to pose or preach; rather, they open and bloom, fresh flowers in a public Zen garden. These fine ancient voices are forever contemporary. As long lost friends, they speak to and through us. As Sung Dynasty poet Chin Kung wrote in his "Living on a Mountain":

Let go of the past.
Why anticipate the future?
Only this day speaks, here and now.
The plum blossoms are ripe, cape-jasmine is sweet.

An essential quality of this writing is its presence, grounded yet alive to the flow of change; another is its humility. "Neither to be praised or blamed" says the Zen poet Miyazawa Kenji of the Zen life and art. While the names and dates of these authors trace a strong lineage, they prove unessential to the direct act of the art, its human gesture and gift. We are indebted to the countless translators of Chinese verse throughout this century who have given us their versions. We humbly offer ours.

Finally, I recall an evening in Ohio not long ago when C. T. Huang, Mei Hui's husband, recited then sang the T'ang poems in the traditional Southern Fu-kien dialect which traces back 1300 years. That night I heard the still, clear beauty of the Chinese Zen, like a Wood Thrush at evening. May these versions which we offer sing with the same clear spirit.

-Larry Smith

RETURN TO THE IDYLLIC LIFE OF THE FARMLAND

-Tao Chien (Tao Yuan Ming) (365-427)

Plant beans at the foot of South Mountain
where the weeds flourish and
   young bean plants are rare.
Early morning, I clear out weeds;
under moonlight, I walk home
   a hoe on my shoulder.
The pathway is narrow,
   and the grasses are high.
Evening dew wets my robe,
yet such dampness doesn't trouble me.
I am as I am—natural to myself.

歸　園　田　居

－　陶　淵　明　(潛)　(東　晉　詩　人)

種　豆　南　山　下　,　草　盛　豆　苗　稀　,

晨　興　理　荒　穢　,　帶　月　荷　鋤　歸　。

道　狹　草　木　長　,　夕　露　霑　我　衣　,

衣　霑　不　足　惜　,　但　使　願　無　違　。

FOREWORD TO BODY, SHADOW, AND SPIRIT

-Tao Chien (Tao Yuan Ming, 365-427)

High and low, ignorant and wise,
all busy seeking immortality—
Such confusion!
Therefore I expose
the pains of both Body and Shadow,
so that Spirit alone may show the way
of Nature, thus dissolving struggle.
I offer this for thoughtful persons
who share my concerns.

形 影 神 （序 ）

- 陶 淵 明 (潛) (東 晉 詩 人)

貴 賤 賢 愚 ，
莫 不 營 營 以 惜 生 ， 斯 甚 惑 焉 ！
故 極 陳 形 影 之 苦 言 ，
神 辨 自 然 以 釋 之 ，
好 事 君 子 共 取 其 心 焉 。

I. THE BODY SPEAKS TO THE SHADOW

-Tao Chien (365-427)

Heaven and Earth exist always;
mountains and rivers without change.
Grass and trees follow their nature
renewed and withered by frosts.
They say men are wise,
and yet they cannot renew.
Just come into the world,
so soon gone, never to return.
Few will miss him,
friends and relatives for a time.
Only when they see his things
do they feel a sorrow.
Lacking immortal magic,
I die like the others.
Please take my kind advice—
When the wine is offered
always take a drink.

形　贈　影

　　　　　－　陶　淵　明　(潛)　(東　晉　詩　人)

天　地　長　不　沒　，　山　川　無　改　時　。

草　木　得　常　理　，　霜　露　榮　悴　之　。

謂　人　最　靈　智　，　獨　復　不　如　茲　。

適　見　在　世　中　，　奄　去　靡　歸　期　。

奚　覺　無　一　人　，　親　識　豈　相　思　。

但　餘　平　生　物　，　舉　目　情　悽　洏　。

我　無　騰　化　術　，　必　爾　不　復　疑　。

願　君　取　吾　言　，　得　酒　莫　苟　辭　。

II. THE SHADOW REPLIES TO THE BODY

-Tao Chien (365-427 AD)

Immortality cannot be reached,
and seeking long life is foolish.
I too wish to wander Paradise
but it is too remote to find.
Since I've met you
we've shared our joy and sorrow.
While you rested in the shadows
we parted for a while.
Yet with the sun's return
we were reunited.
Even so, we cannot remain
side by side forever.
When it comes, we both must go into darkness.
As the body dies, so goes the fame.
This thought burns inside my heart.

Let us labor while we can
to do the good we may.
Wine may in truth dispel our sorrow
but not as well as lasting love.

影 答 形

- 陶 淵 明 (潛) (東 晉 詩 人)

存生不可言，衛生每苦拙。

誠願遊崑華，邈然茲道絕。

與子相遇來，未嘗異悲悅。

憩蔭若暫乖，止日終不別。

此同既難常，黯爾俱時滅。

身沒名亦盡，念之五情熱。

立善有遺愛，胡為不自竭。

酒云能消憂，方此詎不劣。

III. THE SPIRIT SPEAKS

-Tao Chien (365-427 AD)

Our Creator isn't biased;
all things run their course.
Humans become one of the Order of Three
only due to me—the Spirit.
Although we are different,
we are born within each other.
In no way can we escape
our intimacy with evil and good.
The Three Emperors were saintly men—
yet today, where are they?
P'eng lived to a great age,
yet he went at last, still longing to stay.
Old and young, we all are mortal.
Wise or ignorant, no one is saved.
While wine may bring forgetfulness
it also hastens old age.
A good deed is often appreciated,
but who'll praise you after you die?
Such hollow concerns hurt us.
The only way is to follow Nature,
to drift on her Stream of Change
with neither joy nor fear—
And when our time has come,
to go without a trace.

神　釋

- 陶　淵　明（潛）（東　晉　詩　人）

大鈞無私力，萬理自森著。

人爲三才中，豈不以我故。

與君雖異物，生而相依附。

結托善惡同，安得不相語。

三皇大聖人，今復在何處。

彭祖愛永年，欲留不得住。

老少同一死，賢愚無復數。

日醉或能忘，將非促齡具。

立善常所欣，誰當爲汝譽。

甚念傷吾生，正宜委運去。

縱浪大化中，不喜亦不懼。

應盡便須盡，無復獨多慮。

DRINKING

-Tao Yuan Ming (365-427)

My hut settled among neighbors,
    I ignore the noise of horses and carts.

You ask how I get along—
    My mind remains wide,
    so my place is naturally remote.

Picking chrysanthemums at the eastern gate
    I leisurely view South Mountain.
The vapors rise along the valleys,
    groups of birds fly back
        inside each sunset.

Trying to say it, I have
    forgotten the words.

飲　酒

－　陶　淵　明　(陶　潛　‑　晉　詩　人)

結廬在人境，而無車馬喧，

問君何能爾，心遠地自偏。

採菊東籬下，悠然見南山，

山氣日夕佳，飛鳥相與還。

此中有眞意，欲辨已忘言。

SENG CHAO'S DEATH POEM

-Seng Chao (*Monk of Tsin Dynasty, 4th C.)

Of the four elements, I own nothing.
And the five desires bring only emptiness.

For my act of defiance, I receive decapitation—
like chopping spring wind, with a sharp white sword.

[*Note: Poet Seng Chao had refused to serve the violent
kingdom of Fu Chien, and so was put to death; a
striking parallel to more recent events in China.]

僧　肇　遺　偈

-僧　肇（東　晉　僧）

四	大	非	我	有	，
五	蘊	本	來	空	。
掉	頭	挨	白	刃	，
恰	似	斬	春	風	。

MISSING THE WILD GEESE

-Ling Tsang (Sui Dynasty monk, c. 589-
604)

When spring goes, I mourn long,
till fall comes along and relieves my sadness.

Where are those south flying geese?
I miss their shadows across the land.

思　雁

-　靈　藏　(隋　僧)

春　去　心　長　感　，

秋　來　眼　始　寬　。

偏　思　南　下　雁　，

形　影　未　曾　看　。

THE FLOWER AND SEED SEQUENCE

I. POEM

- Bodhidharma (1st Patriarch, ? - 536)

I come to this land
to spread Buddha's seed to those in need.
One flower opens with five petals
and bears fruit naturally.

偈

- 達 摩 (禪 初 祖 ，梁 武 帝 時)

吾 本 來 茲 土 ，

傳 法 渡 迷 情 。

一 花 開 五 葉 ，

結 果 自 然 成 。

II. POEM

- Hui-Ko (2nd Patriarch Zen Master, 486-593)

Because the land is here
we can plant this flower.
Without the original seed
there is no flower.

偈

～ 慧 可 （禪 二 祖 ，隋 朝)

本 來 緣 有 地 ，

因 地 種 花 生 。

本 來 無 有 種 ，

花 亦 不 曾 生 。

III. POEM

-Tseng Tsan (3rd Patriarch Zen Master
500—606)

Though flower seeds come from the ground
they must also go back.
If no one plants them
no flowers will grow.

偈

- 僧 璨 (禪 三 祖 ，隋 朝)

花 種 雖 因 地 ，

從 地 種 花 生 。

若 無 人 下 種 ，

花 種 盡 無 生 。

IV. POEM

-Tao Hsin (4th Patriarch Zen Master
580-651)

Flower seeds have their potential
like the ground's own vitality.
Where good karma is present
flowers grow without intent.

偈

- 道　信（禪　四　祖，初　唐　時）

花　種　有　生　性，

因　地　花　性　生。

大　緣　與　性　合，

當　生　不　生　生。

V. POEM

-Hung Jen (5th Patriarch Zen Master,
601-674)

We sow the seeds with our passion;
those that touch ground will grow.
No feelings, no seeds,
an empty life.

偈

- 弘 忍 (禪 五 祖 ，初 唐 時)

有 情 來 下 種 ，

因 地 果 還 生 。

無 情 亦 無 種 ，

無 性 亦 無 生 。

VI. POEM

-Hui-Neng (6th Patriarch Zen Master
in South, 638-713)

Our seeds are in our hearts and minds.
After a rain, they all will sprout.
Suddenly we feel the flower's growth,
the fruit of enlightenment has emerged.

偈

~ 慧 舷 （禪 南 六 祖 ，唐 初 時）

心 地 含 諸 種 ，

普 雨 悉 皆 萌 。

頓 悟 花 情 已 ，

菩 提 果 自 成 。

VII. POEM

-Huai-Jang (Zen Master 677-744)

Our seeds are in our minds and hearts.
If moistened, all will sprout.
Zen flowers are formless,
in and out of bloom in our hearts.

偈

～ 懷 讓（唐初禪師）

心 地 含 諸 種 ，

遇 澤 悉 皆 萌 。

三 昧 花 無 相 ，

何 壞 復 何 成 。

POEM OF ENLIGHTENMENT

-Shen-Hsiu (6th Patriarch Zen Master in North, 607-706)

The body is the tree of wisdom.
The mind is a clear mirror.
Wipe and polish it constantly.
Keep it free from dust.

示　法　詩

－ 神　秀（北 六 祖 ，隋唐禪師）

身 是 菩 提 樹 ，

心 如 明 鏡 臺 。

時 時 勤 拂 拭 ，

莫 遣 有 塵 埃 。

POEM OF ENLIGHTENMENT

-Hui-Neng (6th Patriarch Zen Master
in South, 638-713)

Wisdom is not a tree,
Nor is the mind a mirror.
Since nothing truly exists,
Where is the need to dust?

示　法　詩

－ 慧　能（南 六 祖 ，唐 初 禪 師）

菩　提　本　非　樹　，

心　境　亦　非　臺　。

本　來　無　一　物　，

何　假　拂　塵　埃　。

FLOWER POEM

-Chih Hsuan (Monk in T'ang Dynasty,
874-888)

The flower blooms,
  a whole tree fills with red.

The flower falls,
  a thousand empty branches.

Only one flower remains,
  for tomorrow's wind.

詠　花

　－　知　玄　（唐　末　僖　宗　時　僧）

花　開　滿　樹　紅　，

花　落　萬　枝　空　。

唯　餘　一　朶　在　，

明　日　定　隨　風　。

A DREAM

-Tao Kai (Monk of T'ang Dynasty,
1107-1110)

Within these many miles,
no one comes.

Yellow covers the mountains
where I fall into autumn.

Awake from a dream on a cliff
I forget old worries at last.

一　夢

- 道 楷 （宋 大 觀 年 間 僧）

數 里 無 人 到 ，

山 黃 始 覺 秋 。

巖 間 一 夢 醒 ，

忘 卻 舊 時 憂 。

LEISURE IN THE AUTUMN NIGHT

-Seng Hsui Mu (Monk in T'ang Dynasy,
c. 898-905)

No longer troubled with things,
who knows such leisure as mine?

I roll up my curtain as in daytime,
move out my couch to face the green mountain.

Wild cranes sleep in the pine trees,
autumn mosses grow after rains.

My trusted friend, a mountain monk,
has answered my letter.

秋　月　閒　居

－ 僧 修 睦（晚 唐 光 化 平 間 僧）

是 事 不 相 關 ， 誰 人 似 此 閒 。

卷 簾 當 白 晝 ， 移 榻 對 青 山 。

野 鶴 眠 松 上 ， 秋 苔 長 雨 間 。

岳 僧 頻 有 信 ， 昨 日 得 書 還 。

SELF-PORTRAIT

-Tan Chiao* (Tang Dynasty, 618-905)

Drawing my portrait, I look for myself,
but find only sadness.
Life becomes a dream of a dream;
this body leaves itself.
Water makes this illusion seem solid;
colored ink dyes this empty world.
Laugh at me if you will,
but I and my portrait
are colored by life's illusion.

[* "Tan Chiao" means a friendship that
appears indifferent yet is as pure as water.]

寫　真

－ 澹 交 (晚 唐 乾 符 平 間 僧)

圖 形 期 自 見 ， 自 見 欲 傷 神 。

已 是 夢 中 夢 ， 更 逢 身 外 身 。

水 花 凝 幻 質 ， 墨 彩 染 空 塵 。

堪 笑 予 兼 爾 ， 俱 爲 未 了 人 。

A FOREWORD FOR MONK CHANG'S
PORTRAIT OF A DRUNKEN MONK

-Huai-Su (Zen Monk, T'ang Dynasty, 618-905)

Everyone hands me wine,
so I never have to pay.
All day in the pine trees
a pot of wine hangs nearby.
I'm not yet a fine cursive calligrapher,
but I'm already quite crazy.
I really look well in this—
portrait of a drunken monk.

題 張 僧 繇 醉 僧 圖

- 懷 素 (唐 上 元 三 年 時 僧)

人 人 送 酒 不 曾 沽 ，

終 日 松 間 挂 一 壺 。

草 聖 欲 成 狂 便 發 ，

真 堪 畫 入 醉 僧 圖 。

FROM COLD MOUNTAIN POEMS

POEM

-Han Shan (Monk, c. 627-649)

Strange the way to Cold Mountain:
without a trace of cart or horse,
unmarked by a winding stream,
in mountain peaks with unknown ridges.

Drops of dew fall from grasses
as the wind sighs through pines;
Lost or confused now,
the body asks the shadow for direction.

詩

- 寒 山 (唐 貞 觀 平 間 僧)

可 笑 寒 山 道 ， 而 無 車 馬 蹤 。

聯 谿 難 記 曲 ， 疊 嶂 不 知 重 。

泣 露 千 般 草 ， 吟 風 一 樣 松 。

此 時 迷 逕 處 ， 形 問 影 如 何 。

POEM

-Han Shan (Monk, 627-649)

Our natural mind like the Autumn moon
Reflected on a clear jade lake.
Nothing like it—
How to explain?

詩

- 寒 山 （唐 貞 觀 平 間 僧）

吾 心 似 秋 月 ，

碧 潭 清 皎 潔 。

無 物 堪 比 倫 ，

教 我 如 何 說 。

POEM

-Han Shan (Monk, 627-649)

We barely reach a hundred years
yet we worry a thousand.
And when we are well
we begin to worry about our children.
We stare down at our field of rice
then up at the mulberry's top,
unable to release our weight.
Why must we wait for the iron weight
to touch bottom in the East Sea
before we rest?

詩

- 寒 山 （唐 貞 觀 年 間 僧）

人 生 不 滿 百 ， 常 懷 千 載 憂 。

自 身 病 始 可 ， 又 為 子 孫 愁 。

下 視 禾 根 土 ， 上 看 桑 樹 頭 。

秤 槌 落 東 海 ， 到 底 始 知 休 。

POEM

-Han Shan (Monk, 627-649)

From a lone mountain peak
In an endless space
I sit humble and alone.
The solitary moon shines on Cold Spring,
yet in the spring I see
only the clear sky.
I sing its song till its end—
and still no Zen.

詩

－ 寒 山 （唐 貞 觀 年 間 僧）

高 高 孤 頂 山 ， 四 顧 極 無 邊 。

獨 坐 無 人 知 ， 孤 月 照 寒 泉 。

泉 中 且 無 月 ， 月 自 在 青 天 。

吟 此 一 曲 歌 ， 歌 終 不 是 禪 。

FREE SPIRIT

-Shih Te (627-649, friend of Han Shan)

Neither to leave, nor to stay,
　　Clear like water.
Neither inside, outside, or between,
　　In one clear drop of water
　　　Everywhere and beyond.

詩

- 拾 得 （唐 貞 觀 年 間 僧）

無 去 無 來 本 湛 然 ，

不 居 內 外 及 中 間 ，

一 顆 水 精 絕 瑕 翳 ，

光 明 透 滿 出 人 天 。

POEM WRITTEN ON THE WALL

-Feng Kan (c. 627-649)

Only this
Nothing more.
No need to dust
No need to sit.

壁 上 詩

- 豐 干 (唐 貞 觀 年 間 僧)

本 來 無 一 物 ，

亦 無 塵 可 拂 。

若 觔 了 達 此 ，

不 用 坐 兀 兀 。

SONG OF ENLIGHTENMENT

-Hsuan Chyuen (Monk, 655-713)

I sought Zen from temples and teachers,
then found it along the way of Tsao Hsi
inside this moment forever.
When walking now, I walk Zen.
When sitting, I sit Zen.
Talking, quiet; moving, stillness,
the calm within.

證 道 歌

- 玄 覺 （初 唐 禪 僧）

尋 師 訪 道 為 參 禪 ，
自 從 認 得 曹 溪 路 ，
了 知 生 死 不 相 干 。
行 亦 禪 ， 坐 亦 禪 ，
語 默 動 靜 體 安 然 。

❖ 39 ❖

SONG OF SUDDEN ENLIGHTENMENT

-Shen Hui (668-760)

When the nothing is something
then the something is nothing.
Walking, stopping, sitting, lying,
the mind is calm within;
each moment a given
the thought empty and free.

頓 悟 無 生 般 若 頌

－ 荷 澤 神 會 (初 唐 禪 師)

無 ， 不 能 無 。

有 ， 不 能 有 。

行 、 住 、 坐 、 臥

心 不 動 搖 ，

一 切 時 中 ， 空 而 無 所 得 。

POEM FROM OLD PANG

-Pang Yun (Zen Master, 806-820)

Yellow leaves fade and fall,
becoming dust.
Neither delusion nor truth
is unchangeable.
Through feelings an old house
fills with autumn colors.
Somehow one becomes
a body of light.

龐 居 士 詩 頌

－ 龐 蘊 （晚 唐 憲 宗 時 禪 師）

黃 葉 飄 零 化 作 塵 ，

本 來 非 妄 亦 非 真 。

有 情 故 宅 含 秋 色 ，

無 名 君 子 湛 然 身 。

RETIRING TO SOUTH MOUNTAIN AT YEAR'S END

-Meng Hao Jan (689-740 AD)

No more petitions to the Capital;
It's time I return to my shabby hut
    on South Mountain.
So little talent—
    a wiser Ruler would discard me.
So often ill—
    I lose touch with old friends.

My gray hair chases my age.
Spring presses hard at year's end.

Holding so much sadness,
    how long will I sleep?
Moonlight through pine trees
    fills my window with emptiness.

歲 暮 歸 南 山

－ 孟 浩 然 （盛 唐 詩 人）

北 闕 休 上 書 ， 南 山 歸 敝 廬 。

不 才 明 主 棄 ， 多 病 故 人 疏 。

白 髮 催 年 老 ， 青 陽 逼 歲 除 。

永 懷 愁 不 寐 ， 松 月 夜 窗 虛 。

SRING DAWN

-Meng Hao Jan (689-740)

I oversleep the spring dawn
hear birds singing everywhere.
How many flowers have fallen
during the wet and windy night?

春　　曉

- 孟 浩 然 （盛 唐 詩 人）

春 眠 不 覺 曉 ，
處 處 聞 啼 鳥 。
夜 來 風 雨 聲 ，
花 落 知 多 少 ？

BIRDS SING IN THE MOUNTAIN STREAM

-Wang Wei (699-759)

In calmness, the sweet olive blossoms fall,
    night echoes of spring hills.
The rising moon startles the mountain birds,
    their song inside the stream.

鳥　鳴　澗

- 王　　維（盛 唐 詩 人）

人　閒　桂　花　落　，
夜　靜　春　山　空　。
月　出　驚　山　鳥　，
時　鳴　春　澗　中　。

HUT AMONG THE BAMBOO

-Wang Wei (699-759)

In the bamboo grove I sit alone,
    strum my lute and whistle long notes.
In the hushed forest, no one hears me,
    only the bright approaching moon.

竹 里 館

- 王 維（盛唐詩人）

獨 坐 幽 篁 裡 ，
彈 琴 復 長 嘯 。
深 林 人 不 知 ，
明 月 來 相 照 。

VILLAGE OF THE DEER STOCKADE

-Wang Wei (699-759)

On this lone mountain, I see no one,
yet I hear an echo of voices.
The sun sets in dense woods
and shines above on green moss.

鹿　柴

－王　維（盛唐詩人）

空　山　不　見　人　，
但　聞　人　語　響　。
返　景　入　深　林　，
復　照　青　苔　上　。

WEN-APRICOT HUT

-Wang Wei (699-759)

They have cut wen-apricot for beams,
and knit lemon grass for their roof.
Why must clouds among the ridgepoles
bring our human rains?

文　杏　館

- 王　　維（盛唐詩人）

文　杏　裁　爲　梁　，
香　茅　結　爲　宇　。
不　知　棟　裡　雲　，
去　作　人　間　雨　。

HIBISCUS VILLAGE

-Wang Wei (699-759 AD)

Hibiscus buds on the tree tops
shoot red pods all over the mountain.
Alone near the quiet stream
the blossoms open and fall.

辛　夷　塢

－王　　維（盛唐詩人）

木　末　芙　蓉　花　，

山　中　發　紅　萼　。

澗　戶　寂　無　人　，

紛　紛　開　且　落　。

A POEM

-Wang Wei (699-759 AD)

You've come from my hometown
so you know the village news.
Tell me, please,
was the winter plum tree near my window
in flower on the day you left?

雜　詩

－ 王　　維 （盛 唐 詩 人）

君　自　故　鄉　來　，

應　知　故　鄉　事　。

來　日　綺　窗　前　，

寒　梅　著　花　未　？

FROM MY COUNTRY RETREAT
BY THE RIVER WANG AFTER HEAVY RAIN

-Wang Wei (699-759 AD)

Rainy days in this empty woods,
    smoke floats up from chimneys
where they stew vegetables and steam millet
    to send to the far acres.

Above these flooded fields
    a white egret glides;
in the green summer woods
    a golden oriole sings.

I meditate these mountains,
    contemplate the morning glory.
For my meal under pines
    I gather dewy ferns.

An old farmer now, I've abandoned
    the struggle for gain—
So why do those seagulls
    mock me still?

積雨輞川莊作

－王　維（盛唐詩人）

積雨空林煙火遲，

蒸藜炊黍餉東菑。

漠漠水田飛白鷺，

陰陰夏木囀黃鸝。

山中習靜觀朝槿，

松下清齋折露葵。

野老與人爭席罷，

海鷗何事更相疑。

❖ 51 ❖

IN THE MOUNTAIN

-Wang Wei (699-759)

The white stones appear in the Ching
    stream.
A few red leaves in the cold sky.
No rain on these mountain trails,
yet my robe is damp from passing here.

山　中

- 王　　維（盛唐詩人）

荆　溪　白　石　出　，
天　寒　紅　葉　稀　。
山　路　元　無　雨　，
空　翠　濕　人　衣　。

MY RETREAT ON SOUTH MOUNTAIN

-Wang Wei (699-759)

In middle age
    I came to love the Way.
 Later, I built my home
    on South Mountain.

When impulse stirs
    I wander there,
And enjoy alone
    this time and place.
I walk to where
    the river begins,
Sit inside the moment,
    watch the clouds begin to rise.

Sometimes I meet
    the old woodcutter,
And we talk and laugh together
    forgetting to go home.

終　南　別　業

－　王　維（盛　唐　詩　人）

中 歲 頗 好 道 ， 晚 家 南 山 陲 。

興 來 每 獨 往 ， 勝 事 空 自 知 。

行 到 水 窮 處 ， 坐 看 雲 起 時 。

偶 然 值 林 叟 ， 談 笑 無 還 期 。

NIGHT THOUGHTS

-Li Po (701-762 AD)

Before my bed, a bright shining moon.
It seems like frost covering the earthen
        floor.
I raise my head to gaze at the clear moon;
then bow to thoughts of my home town.

夜　思

- 李　白（盛　唐　詩　人）

床　前　明　月　光　，

疑　是　地　上　霜　。

舉　頭　望　明　月　，

低　頭　思　故　鄉　。

LOOKING FOR MASTER CHANG AT SOUTH RIVER

-Liu Chang Ching (709-780)

All along the trail of moss,
 I followed your wooden shoeprints.
White clouds hung around your little island
 where spring grass hid your unlocked door.
I enjoyed the colors of pines after rain
 and reached the river's source
 along the mountain trail.
Facing the stream and the flowers
 I came inside a sense of Zen,
yet cannot find the words.

尋 南 溪 常 道 士

－ 劉 長 卿 (盛 唐 詩 人)

一 路 經 行 處 ， 莓 苔 見 屐 痕 。

白 雲 依 靜 渚 ， 春 草 閉 閑 門 。

過 雨 看 松 色 ， 隨 山 到 水 源 。

溪 花 與 禪 意 ， 相 對 亦 忘 言 。

RESPONSE TO CHANG YEN'S POEM—
AUTUMN NIGHT

-Han Hung (c. 754)

The wind against long bamboo
        in an early autumn night;
an empty city,
    fills with soft moonlight.
And in the sky,
    wild geese cross the Milky Way.

My neighbor's washing stone
    rolls on, deeper into night.
One knows late autumn
    has already come.
Yet I keep our promise to write,
    and will sleep another time.
My friend, I love so much
    your fine cadenced lines,
I barely notice the crows
    are cawing for the dawn.

酬 程 延 秋 夜 即 事 見 贈

- 翰 翃 (盛 唐 詩 人)

長 篁 迎 風 早 ， 空 城 澹 月 華 。

星 河 秋 一 雁 ， 砧 杵 夜 千 家 。

節 候 看 應 晚 ， 心 期 臥 亦 賒 。

向 來 吟 秀 句 ， 不 覺 已 鳴 鴉 。

CH'IN

-Yin Luan (Monk of late T'ang Dynasty)

Upon these seven strings I place my feelings
with the waters of a mountain stream,
the winds inside the pines—
alive to these old fingers.
My friends are few so I wonder
does anyone hear my song?

琴

— 隱 巒（晚 唐 僧）

七 條 絲 上 寄 深 意 ，

澗 水 松 風 生 十 指 。

自 乃 知 音 猶 尚 稀 ，

欲 敎 更 入 何 人 耳 ？

WATCHING SNOW DRIFTS ON SOUTH MOUNTAIN

-Tsu Yung (c. 713-741)

The northern shadows of South Mountain
    are more than beautiful.
Its snowy peak floats through
    the crest of clouds.
A clear sky gleams
    to the forest's edge.
Yet in the city of Chang An,
    a cold dusk comes on.

終 南 望 餘 雪

－ 祖 詠 （唐 開 元 平 間 詩 人）

終 南 陰 嶺 秀 ，
積 雪 浮 雲 端 。
林 表 明 霽 色 ，
城 中 增 暮 寒 。

MOONLIT NIGHT

-Liu Fang-Ping (8th Century)

Deep moonlight
 paints half my house.
The Big Dipper slopes;
 the Great Bear bends down.
Tonight I notice
 the warm air of spring.
The insects begin chirping
 through the green gauze of my window.

月　夜

－ 劉 方 平
（中唐大曆貞元平間詩人）

更 深 月 色 半 人 家 ，

北 斗 闌 干 南 斗 斜 。

今 夜 偏 知 春 氣 暖 ，

蟲 聲 新 透 綠 窗 紗 。

WELCOME

-Tu Fu (712-770)

North and South, my house is surrounded by
　　　spring water.
Only the seagulls visit each day.
No need to clean the path through my garden,
Yet today I have opened my thatched hut for you.
Too far from town and without rich food,
I can offer only this cheap wine.
If you don't mind, I'll call over my old neighbors
To help us finish this jug of wine.

客　　　至

－　杜　甫　（盛唐詩人）

舍南舍北皆春水，但見羣鷗日日來。

花逕不曾緣客掃，蓬門今始為君開。

盤飧市遠無兼味，尊酒家貧只舊醅。

肯與鄰翁相對飲，隔籬呼取盡餘杯。

ASCENDING

-Tu Fu (712-770)

Strong winds across the sky,
the howling of apes.
Clear island of white sands,
the hovering birds.
Leaves fall in the deep forest;
the waters of the Yangtze River roll on.
Traveling so far and so often,
I feel the sadness of autumn.
So often ill and alone,
yet still I want to climb the heights.
Not blaming a life of struggle,
yet I hate my graying hair.
Frustrated, I throw down
my cup of cloudy wine.

九 日 登 高

— 杜 甫 （ 盛 唐 詩 人 ）

風 急 天 高 猿 嘯 哀 ， 渚 清 沙 白 鳥 飛 迴 。

無 邊 落 木 蕭 蕭 下 ， 不 盡 長 江 滾 滾 來 。

萬 里 悲 秋 常 作 客 ， 百 年 多 病 獨 登 臺 。

艱 難 苦 恨 繁 霜 鬢 ， 潦 倒 新 停 濁 酒 杯 。

A FLOWER NOT A FLOWER

-Pai-Chu-I (772-846)

Flowers not flowers, fog not fog;
it comes at midnight, goes at dawn.
Arriving like a spring dream,
leaving like the morning clouds—
no way to hold it.

花　非　花

－　白　居　易　（中　唐　詩　人）

花 非 花 ， 霧 非 霧 ，

夜 半 來 ， 天 明 去 ，

來 如 春 夢 幾 多 時 ，

去 似 朝 雲 無 覓 處 。

READING A POEM OF YUAN-CHIU IN A BOAT

-Pai-Chu-I (772-846)

Holding the scroll
    I study your poem
finishing just before dawn,
    the lamplight almost gone.
My eyes tired,
    I put out the light
        and sit in the dark
while winds push waves
    against my little boat.

舟 中 讀 元 九 詩

－ 白 居 易 （中 唐 詩 人）

把 君 詩 卷 細 細 讀 ，

詩 盡 燈 殘 天 未 明 。

眼 痛 滅 燈 猶 闇 坐 ，

逆 風 吹 浪 打 船 聲 。

RIVER SNOW

-Liu-Tsung-Yuan (773-819 AD)

In a thousand mountains
   the birds have ceased to fly.
On countless trails
   footprints have disappeared.
Only a solitary boatman
   in a straw cape and hat
fishes the snow
   of the icy river.

江　雪

～ 柳宗元（中唐詩人）

千　山　鳥　飛　絕　，

萬　逕　人　蹤　滅　。

孤　舟　簑　笠　翁　，

獨　釣　寒　江　雪　。

A THOUGHT AT YEAR'S END

- Wang Chien (T'ang Dynasty, 766—)

Everyone wants to be young forever,
yet even my neighbors are turning grey.
I try hard to avoid stress
yet there's no way to stop this aging.
I think about building a hermit's cottage
and should plant those pine trees now.
From this day I swear to make my life
bloom for twenty years more.

歲 晚 自 感

- 王 建 (中 唐 大 曆 年 間 詩 人)

人 皆 欲 得 長 年 少 ， 無 那 排 門 白 髮 催 。
一 向 破 除 愁 不 盡 ， 百 方 迴 避 老 須 來 。
草 堂 未 辨 終 須 置 ， 松 樹 難 成 亦 且 栽 。
瀝 酒 願 從 今 日 後 ， 更 逢 二 十 度 花 開 。

THIS HUMAN LIFE

-Chiao Jan (Monk in T'ang Dynasty
c. 785-805)

If this human life is a hundred years,
then I have passed away half.
My talent is so poor and helpless,
I fished at Eastern Sea
without even a turtle bite.
I sit on this decaying rock now
at Southern Mountain.

人　生

- 皎　然 （中唐貞元年間僧）

人 生 百 歲 我 過 半 ，

天 生 才 定 不 可 換 。

東 海 釣 鼇 鼇 不 食 ，

南 山 坐 石 石 欲 爛 。

MOON ON WATER

-Chiao Jan (Monk in T'ang Dynasty,
c. 785-895)

Each night, I gaze upon a pond,
a Zen body sitting beside a moon.
Nothing is really there and yet
it is all so clear and bright
I cannot describe it.
If you would know the empty mind
your own mind must be as clear and bright
as this full moon upon the water.

水　月

－ 皎　然（中唐貞元平間詩人）

夜 夜 池 上 觀 ， 禪 身 坐 月 邊 。

虛 無 色 可 取 ， 皎 潔 意 難 傳 。

若 向 空 心 了 ， 長 如 影 正 圓 。

MY STAY AT A MOUNTAIN WITH A MOON

-Chiao Jan (Monk in T'ang Dynasty,
c. 785-805)

Night after night I sit on this mountain
under the moon alone.
Yet tonight you are with me
and the moon and mountain disappear.

待　山　月

- 皎　然　（中唐貞元年間僧）

夜　夜　憶　故　人　，

長　敎　山　月　待　。

今　宵　故　人　來　，

山　月　知　何　在　。

SERMON ON LARGE SELF AT HU-NAN PROVINCE

-Chaio Jan (Monk in Tan'g Dynasty,
785-805)

Not yet to the shore of empty mind,
I reach in vain for the unmoored boat.
At East Mountain top, white clouds
at year's end, always calm.

湖 南 蘭 若 示 大 乘 諸 公

- 皎　然　(中唐貞元平間僧)

未　到　無　爲　岸　，

空　憐　不　繋　舟　。

東　山　白　雲　意　，

歲　晚　尚　悠　悠　。

DEDICATION FOR A ZEN MONASTERY

-Yu Fu (T'ang Dynasty, 785-805)

No flower blooms, yet the land is sweet.
The cranes make the pines look more tall.
Why must one be lonely in this place
Where all the monks are old friends?

題　禪　院

~ 喻　鳧　（晚唐開城平間詩人）

無　花　地　亦　香　，

有　鶴　松　多　直　。

向　此　奚　必　孤　，

山　僧　盡　相　識　。

ANCHORED FOR THE NIGHT AT MAPLE BRIDGE

-Chang Chi (T'ang Dynasty, -d. 789)

Crows caw as the moon sets,
 the sky's frost covering all;
River maples from the boat's lantern
 Shiver in the sleepless night.
Just beyond the city of Ku Su
 lies Cold Mountain monastery.
At midnight the voice of its bell
 reaches this traveller's boat.

楓 橋 夜 泊

- 張　繼 （中唐貞元平間詩人）

月 落 烏 啼 霜 滿 天 ，

江 楓 漁 火 對 愁 眠 。

姑 蘇 城 外 寒 山 寺 ，

夜 半 鐘 聲 到 客 船 。

ON VISITING A HERMIT AND NOT
FINDING HIM AT HOME

-Wu Pen (Chia Tao) [Monk of T'ang Dynasty,
793-865)

Under a pine tree I ask a houseboy,
who says "My master is gathering herbs."
Somewhere on the mountainside you—
lost to me in deep clouds.

尋 隱 者 不 遇

－ 賈 島 （中唐詩人，曾為僧，名無本）

松 下 問 童 子 ，

言 師 採 藥 去 。

只 在 此 山 中 ，

雲 深 不 知 處 。

A POEM FOR DUKE WANG (Short Version)

-Kuan Hsiu (832-912)

With one bottle, one alms bowl,
    I reach old age.
A thousand rivers, a thousand mountains,
    I arrive at last.

（節錄）獻 蜀 王 建

　　　~貫 休（晚 唐 高 僧）

一 瓶 一 缽 垂 垂 老，

萬 水 千 山 得 得 來 。

THINKING OF MASTER CHIH-TI

-Kuan Hsiu (832-921)

Holding the pen I think of you
while orioles sing in the yard.
If only we lived in one place
I should not be missing you.
Melted snow floods under
      the door of my room;
spring thunder breaks the
      branches of my trees.
So many things in my life I share
with you and these white clouds.

懷 智 體 道 人

- 貫 休 (晚 唐 高 僧)

把 筆 懷 吾 友 ， 庭 鶯 百 囀 時 。

惟 應 一 處 住 ， 方 得 不 相 思 。

雪 水 淹 門 閫 ， 春 雷 折 樹 枝 。

平 生 無 限 事 ， 不 獨 白 雲 知 。

POEM (WHILE WALKING WITH THE EMPEROR)

-Fa Yen (Ching Liang, 885-958)

Holding my sweater and facing the fragrant peony,
I sense how different our viewpoints are.
Someday our hair will turn gray,
yet the flowers will be this red each year;
following the morning dew, each blooms gorgeously
then their sweet scent is chased by the evening winds.
Why wait till they have withered and fallen
to understand such emptiness?

無　題

- 法 眼 清 涼 文 益 （晚唐高僧）

擁 毳 對 芳 叢 ， 由 來 趣 不 同 。

髮 從 今 日 白 ， 花 是 去 年 紅 。

艷 冶 隨 朝 露 ， 馨 香 逐 晚 風 。

何 須 待 零 落 ， 然 後 始 知 空 。

POEM

-Fa Yen (Ching Liang, 885-958)

Hidden birds sing as cool and clear
as a bamboo forest.
Between swinging willows sun beams
glimmer like golden threads.
Clouds return to this calm valley.
The winds carry the fragrance of almonds.
By sitting alone all day long
I clear my mind of a thousand thoughts.
To speak of this is beyond our words;
only by sitting under the quiet forest
can we ever understand.

無　題

－法眼清涼文益（晚唐高僧）

幽鳥語如簧，柳搖金線長。

雲歸山谷靜，風送杏花香。

永日蕭然坐，澄心萬慮忘。

欲言言不及，林下好商量。

MEETING AN OLDER MAN

- Yin Luan* (late T'ang Dynasty, 847-906)

On the road I meet an old man,
his hair light at the temples like snow.
One mile, two miles he walks,
four times, five times, and then
he pauses for a rest.

[*"Yin Luan" also means to live secluded
in the mountains]

逢 老 人

- 隱 巒 (晚 唐 僧)

路 逢 一 老 翁 ，
兩 鬢 白 如 雪 。
一 里 二 里 行 ，
四 回 五 回 歇 。

DIVERTING MYSELF

-Kuei Jen (Monk. c. 847-906)

Day after day
    I work with a rhyme.
The spring, the fall,
    let it be.

Once a good line
    comes out of my head,
Nothing can bother me.

The falling rain
    brings flowers to the steps;
The blowing wind
    bends bamboo towards the tower.

If I don't write these things,
    my hair will still turn gray.

So I write them
    for all these gray hairs.

自　遣

- 歸 仁 （晚 唐 僧）

日 日 爲 詩 苦 ， 誰 論 春 與 秋 。

一 聯 如 得 意 ， 萬 事 總 忘 憂 。

雨 墜 花 臨 砌 ， 風 吹 竹 近 樓 。

不 吟 頭 也 白 ， 任 白 此 生 頭 。

A SIGH FOR MYSELF

-Fa Yuan (Sung Dynasty monk, 960-1278)

A lone boat floats on waves
    in the quiet night.
Reeds stand along the shore
    against a bright moon.
All the golden fishes have gone
    down deep into the lake.
Leaving this solitary fisherman
    holding his empty pole.

自 嘆

- 法 遠 （宋 初 僧）

孤 舟 夜 靜 泛 波 瀾 ，

兩 岸 蘆 花 對 月 圓 。

金 鱗 自 入 深 潭 去 ，

空 使 漁 翁 執 釣 竿 。

COLD NIGHT

-Tu Hsiao Shan (Sung Dynasty, 960-1278)

On a cold night you come and
I serve tea instead of wine.
On the bamboo stove water boils
as the fire glows red.
Before the window the moon
is as bright as ever.
Yet tonight among these plum blossoms
somehow more beautiful.

寒　夜

－杜小山（宋光宗時詩人）

寒夜客來茶當酒，

竹爐湯沸火初紅。

尋常一樣窗前月，

纔有梅花便不同。

AWAKENING FROM A NAP

-T'sung Yeuh (Monk of Sung Dynasty,
960-1278)

Within these many miles
    I see no one.

Yellow appears on the mountains
    and I notice the fall.

Awake from a nap on a cliff,
    I forget to worry at last.

一　覺　醒

- 淙　悅　(宋　末　僧)

數　里　無　人　到　，

山　黃　始　識　秋　。

巖　間　一　覺　醒　，

忘　卻　百　年　憂　。

IN PRAISE OF CHANG SHA'S
"A TRIP TO THE MOUNTAIN"

-Hseuh Tou (980-1052 AD)

The earth is free of dust.
Who cannot see?
Follow the sweet grasses to the mountain top,
Then chase home the falling pedals.
Slim cranes raise their heads toward the cold woods;
Wild apes howl on the old terrace.
Master Chang Sha's wise lines
Say it all.

頌 長 沙 遊 山 詩

- 雪 竇 重 顯 (宋初高僧)

大 地 絕 纖 埃 ， 何 人 眼 不 開 。

始 隨 芳 草 去 ， 又 逐 落 花 回 。

羸 鶴 翹 寒 木 ， 狂 猿 嘯 古 臺 。

長 沙 無 限 意 ，

咄 ！ 掘 地 更 深 埋 ！

AN ALLEGORY

-Wang An Shih (1021-1086 AD, known as
                "Half Mountain Man")

Often I doubt the Buddhist way,
that nothing truly exists.
So by practicing meditation
Do I fool myself?
They say all natural things
speak the same Buddhist truth,
yet in meditation at the wall
I cannot save myself.

寓　言

－ 王　安　石 (半山居士，宋仁宗時詩人)

本　來　無　物　使　人　疑　，

卻　無　參　禪　買　得　癡　。

聞　道　無　情　皈　說　法　，

面　墻　終　日　妄　尋　思　。

LATE SPRING

-Wang An Shih (1021-86 AD,
  known as "Half Mountain Man")

Countless red petals fall to earth.
Misty trees beside the stream shine greenly.
Only the willow catkins understand spring winds
running off together into clear blue sky.

暮　春

~王　安　石(半山居士，宋仁宗時詩人)

無 限 殘 紅 著 地 飛 ，

溪 頭 煙 樹 翠 相 圍 。

楊 花 獨 得 東 風 意 ，

相 逐 晴 空 去 不 歸 。

MOUNT LU POEMS

-Su Shih (1031-1101)

I. An Inscription Poem from the Wall
    of Hsi-Lin Temple

At the horizon the mountain seems huge;
up close it's a towering peak.
From far, near, high, or low, it's not the same.
What is the true face of Mount Lu?
On a mountain, one cannot see the mountain.

廬　山　－　題　西　林　壁

－　蘇　軾（蘇東坡，宋仁宗時詩人）

橫　看　成　嶺　側　成　峰，

遠　近　高　低　各　不　同。

不　識　廬　山　眞　面　目，

唯　緣　身　在　此　山　中。

II. POEM

-Su Shih (1031-1101)

Mist and fog and rain
 like the waves of the River Che.
Mount Lu and the River Che, each ever-changing
 like our endless passions.
Then all changes and fog and the rain
 are no more.
Mount Lu's fog and rain—
 as fair as the waves of River Che.

廬　山

－ 蘇　軾（蘇東坡，宋仁宗時詩人）

廬 山 煙 雨 浙 江 潮 ，

未 到 千 般 恨 不 消 。

到 得 還 來 無 別 事 ，

廬 山 煙 雨 浙 江 潮 。

III   For the Master of Tung-Lin Temple

-Su Shih (1031-1101)

The sounds of streams are Buddha's speech.
The colored mountains are Buddha's pure body.
Night brings eighty-four thousand poems of Buddha.
Listen, and someday you may awaken.

贈 東 林 總 長 老

-- 蘇　軾 (蘇東坡，宋仁宗時詩人)

溪 聲 便 是 廣 長 舌 ，

山 色 豈 非 清 淨 身 。

夜 來 八 萬 四 千 偈 ，

他 日 如 何 舉 世 人 。

MOUNTAIN JOURNAL

-Chang Ling (Monk of Sung Dynasty,
1065-1123)

Mountain living is cold and slow,
a lone monkey staring at a skinny crane.
Yet I add more clothes and do not mind.
No need to search for other Buddhas;
stirring the grasses I find an orchid of peace.
My heart opens as a valley full of echoes;
my mind plays the stringless lute.
If you say all this is nothing,
then I know the Master's fool.

山 居

- 長 靈 守 卓 (宋中葉時僧)

孤 猿 瘦 鶴 冷 相 看 ， 百 納 三 衣 任 歲 寒 。

未 擬 將 心 求 別 佛 ， 曾 因 撥 草 見 幽 蘭 。

誰 為 虛 谷 呼 皆 應 ， 自 許 無 絃 密 可 彈 。

若 謂 本 來 無 一 物 ， 知 公 親 被 祖 師 謾 。

FREE FROM NEW YEAR'S GREETING

-Tao Kai (Sung Dynasty monk, 1065-1123)

The sun rises; the sun sets.
Watch it and see.
River and moon
Pine trees and wind—
all old poems to me.
Who needs words for the New Year!

歲 暮 免 人 事

- 道 楷 （宋中葉時僧）

日 出 東 方 夜 落 西 ，

急 須 著 眼 莫 遲 疑 。

新 平 不 用 來 相 賀 ，

江 月 松 風 似 舊 詩 。

A POEM FOR AUTUMN

-Kuo-Yin (Sung Dynasty, c. 1111)

A piece of mind as clear as the sky
where clouds float freely into all.
This quiet night I do not lean toward sleep
but listen for leaves falling in my yard.

秋 日 即 興

- 郭 印 （宋政和年間詩人）

一 片 澄 心 似 太 清 ，

浮 雲 了 不 礙 虛 明 。

夜 深 人 寂 渾 無 寐 ，

時 聽 空 庭 落 葉 聲 。

POEM

-Lin Chi Chung (c. 1119, Sung Dynasty)

Don't say that only clear water mirrors the moon.
Muddy water also reflects the sky.
Watch, after wind has settled and the waves are calm,
for a wonderful moon, as lovely as before.

止 鑑 堂 詩

- 林 季 仲 (宋宣和平間詩人)

莫 道 水 清 偏 得 月 ，

湏 知 水 濁 亦 全 天 。

請 看 風 定 波 平 後 ，

一 顆 靈 珠 依 舊 圓 。

SAILING A SMALL BOAT ON A DAM

-Chu Hsi (1130-1200, Sung Dynasty)

With a straw cape I huddled last night
in the corner of my little boat.
What else could I do on so dark a night?
The winds blew waves all over the river.

This morning I roll up my canvas
to take a peek:
Green mountain and trees
everywhere again.

水 口 汀 舟

- 朱　熹（宋紹興平間哲人）

昨 夜 扁 舟 雨 一 簑 ，

滿 江 風 浪 夜 如 何 ？

今 朝 試 卷 孤 蓬 看 ，

依 舊 青 山 綠 樹 多 。

A COMMENT ON READING #1

-Chu-Hsi (Sung Dynasty philosopher,
1130-1200)

A half acre pond opens like a mirror.
Images of sky and clouds ripple together.
You ask how it can be so clear.
Because fresh water flows through it.

觀 書 有 感 #1

- 朱 熹 (宋紹興年間哲人)

半 畝 方 塘 一 鑑 開 ,

天 光 雲 影 共 徘 徊 。

問 渠 那 得 清 如 許 ,

為 有 源 頭 活 水 來 。

A COMMENT ON READING #2

-Chu-Hsi (Sung Dynasty philosopher,
1130-1200)

Last night's spring water has raised the river,
forcing a ship to move like a feather.
Moving it before was a wasted effort;
today it sails freely in the river's flow.

觀 書 有 感　#2

- 朱　熹 （宋紹興年間哲人）

昨 夜 江 邊 春 水 生 ，

蒙 衝 巨 艦 一 毛 輕 。

向 來 枉 費 推 移 力 ，

此 日 中 流 自 在 行 。

ON NAN-CH'UAN'S "TAO IS ORDINARY MIND"

-Wu-Men-Hui-Kai (Zen Master, 1183-1260)

Spring has its hundred flowers,
  Autumn its many moons.
Summer has cool winds,
  Winter its snow.
If useless thoughts do not
  cloud your mind,
Each day is the best of your life.

頌 "南 泉 平 常 心 是 道"

- 無 門 慧 開 (宋理宗時高僧)

春 有 百 花 秋 有 月，

夏 有 涼 風 冬 有 雪 。

若 無 閒 事 挂 心 頭，

便 是 人 間 好 時 節 。

TO MASTER YING

-Yuan, Hao-Wen (1190-1257 AD)

Turning from worldly things
I buy some wine.
Nothing bothers me here
neither honor nor blame.
Only you to share my pains and sorrows.
And why must two grey-haired friends
live so far apart?
Even green mountains under Ping-Chou's moon
cry for us tonight.
Old friend, I miss you so much
that I sing to Tang-Hsiu
the poem of bright clouds.

寄 英 上 人

- 元 好 問 （元朝中葉詩人）

世 事 都 銷 酒 半 醺 ， 已 將 度 外 置 紛 紜 。

乍 賢 乍 佞 誰 爲 我 ， 同 病 同 憂 只 有 君 。

白 首 共 傷 千 里 別 ， 青 山 眞 得 幾 時 分 。

相 思 後 夜 幷 州 月 ， 卻 爲 湯 休 賦 碧 雲 。

AUTUMN THOUGHTS

-Ma Chih Yuan (1250-1324?)

Withered vine, old tree, dark crow;
crossing bridge, flowing water, old houses;
worn path, West wind, thin horse;
A China sun sets in the West,
heartbroken at sky's edge.

天 淨 沙 --- 秋 思

- 馬 致 遠 (元朝中葉詩人)

枯 藤 、 老 樹 、 昏 鴉 、

小 橋 、 流 水 、 人 家 、

古 道 、 西 風 、 瘦 馬 、

夕 陽 西 下 ;

斷 腸 人 在 天 涯 。

RESPONDING TO YUNG-MING'S ZEN RHYMES

-Wu Chen Hsien Tu (Sung Dynasty
1265-1334)

Few people reach such clear, cool clouds.
I suddenly realize how all things and I are one.
Red peach and white plum flowers—
the essence of Nature.
The oriole's song and the swallow's flight
reveal such delicate points.
In streams rising after new rains
the fish are dense.
Old clouds return to the ravine
in soft sunlight.
In silence I share all of this
with my good friends,
no thought of right or wrong.

和 永 明 禪 師 韻

- 無 見 先 睹 （宋 末 僧）

清 冷 雲 中 到 者 稀 ， 廓 然 物 我 自 同 歸 。

桃 紅 李 白 資 眞 諦 ， 燕 語 鶯 啼 闡 妙 機 。

新 水 漲 溪 魚 影 密 ， 宿 雲 歸 洞 日 光 微 。

祇 將 一 默 酬 知 已 ， 是 不 是 兮 非 不 非 。

LIVING ON A MOUNTAIN

-Chin Kung (Monk in Sung Dynasty,
1272-1352)

Let go of the past.
Why anticipate the future?
Only this day speaks, here and now.
The plums are ripe, cape-jasmine is sweet.

山　居

- 清　珙（宋末僧）

過去事已過去了，

未來不必預思量。

只今便道即今句，

梅子熟時栀子香。

CHIN KUNG'S BEQUEST POEM

-Chin Kung (Monk of Sung Dynasty,
1272-1352)

Green mountains won't preserve a body,
So why bury the dead in mountain soil?

Look at me, unable to meditate now,
a sack of firewood, before and after I die.

清 珙 遺 偈

- 清 珙 (宋 末 僧)

青 山 不 著 死 屍 骸 ，

死 了 何 湏 掘 土 埋 ？

顧 我 也 無 三 昧 火 ，

先 前 絕 後 一 堆 柴 。

TRAVELLING SOUTH

-Cheng Mien (Monk of Ming Dynasty,
c.14th C.)

Under the glowing sunset, I walked with a stick,
no time for sky watching.
Three years I've traveled south on river road
just to find this cool, clear spring.

南　下

- 正　勉 (明朝中葉?僧)

策 杖 逡 巡 夕 照 邊 ，

無 心 佇 足 望 蒼 天 。

三 春 僕 僕 江 南 路 ，

為 訪 清 冷 一 窟 泉 。

ON A MONK MENDING HIS CLOTHES

-Ta Tung (Ming Dynasty monk, 1368-1390)

Among vast fields of people,
he diligently mends his robes.
Forgetting how all people resemble him,
why distinguish between
the large and small self?

補 衲 僧

- 大 同 （元末明洪武初僧）

莽 莽 十 方 客 ，

孜 孜 補 衲 僧 。

不 知 人 我 相 ，

焉 別 大 小 乘 。

MOUNTAIN POEM

-Han Shan Te Ching (Monk of Ming Dynasty
1546-1623)

Life rolls along like this dusty world.
And now I must leave my town.
Each day I look back at my distant home,
And the dusky sky bathed in red.

山 居 偶 成

- 憨 山 德 清 （明末僧）

滾 滾 紅 塵 世 路 長 ，

不 知 何 事 走 他 鄉 。

回 頭 日 望 家 鄉 遠 ，

滿 目 空 雲 帶 夕 陽 。

MOUNTAIN LIVING

-Han Shan Te Ching (Monk of Ming Dynasty,
1546-1623)

Tonight so deep and cold
I sit alone, bored with Zen.

I stir up the last ashes
but no spark ignites.

Suddenly I hear temple bells
tolling to a roar,

Then clear rhyming tones
cover this frosted world.

山 居

- 憨 山 德 清 (明末僧)

夜 深 獨 坐 事 枯 禪 ,

撥 盡 寒 灰 火 不 燃 。

忽 聽 樓 頭 鐘 磬 發 ,

一 聲 清 韻 滿 霜 天 。

MOUNTAIN JOURNAL

-Han Shan Te Ching (1546-1623, not to be
confused with earlier Han Shan)

Flowing water, outside sound;
bright moon, beyond color.
Sounds and beauty—not essence.
Who can understand?

憶 山 居

- 憨 山 德 清 （明末僧）

流 水 不 是 聲 ，

明 月 元 非 色 。

聲 色 不 相 關 ，

此 境 誰 會 得 。

REPLY TO MR. LEE, ALMS GIVER

-Fo-E (Monk of Ching Dynasty,
7th Century)

Why claim that Buddha
is not on high mountain?
If Buddha is in your heart
why search for his traces elsewhere?
Crossing a river or climbing a mountain
will not help you find him.
Much better to sit and meditate,
worship your own pure heart.

答 李 施 主

- 佛 喬 (清初僧)

誰 云 鷲 嶺 佛 難 逢 ，

佛 在 心 中 那 有 蹤 ？

涉 水 盤 山 空 負 累 ，

不 如 端 坐 自 家 供 。

THIS BUSY STRUGGLE

-Shih Lien (alias "Not I," Monk in Ching
Dynasty, 1644-1908)

Turning clouds, swirling waters,
run their own way
regardless of rice grains or mulberry.
People are even more busy
in endless struggles,
struggles with each other
for empty dreams.

爭　忙

－石　蓮　（清初僧）

但 見 雲 忙 水 亦 忙 ，

所 忙 不 在 稻 梁 桑 。

芸 芸 更 是 忙 無 既 ，

波 此 爭 忙 夢 一 場 。

SITTING IN THE SUN

-Shu-Liang (Monk of Ching Dynasty, 1604-1908)

The frost melts, stairs in the yard
are covered with leaves.
A lovely sun warms my shabby cottage,
making me so comfortable I fall asleep
unknowing my book drops from my hands.

坐　曝

～ 叔　良　（清僧）

霜 乾 落 葉 滿 庭 除 ，

愛 日 烘 人 入 敝 廬 。

暖 透 四 肢 渾 坐 睡 ，

不 知 墜 卻 手 中 書 。

TO MASTER I-CHUAN

-Hsu-Yun (1840-1943)

I have stayed in this mountain for decades
so that grey hair covers my head.
Heartfelt poems touch deep my bones,
while talk of isolation
fills me with helpless tears.
I have wasted my life doing nothing,
traveling home only in dreams.
How can I bear to hear this rain at my eaves
drop after drop, tone after tone, without end?

贈 一 全 上 人

- 虛 雲 (近代禪師)

一 臥 溪 山 數 十 秋 ， 不 知 白 髮 已 盈 頭 。

詩 舷 入 骨 情 多 碎 ， 話 到 離 羣 淚 自 流 。

好 事 竟 從 閒 裡 過 ， 故 鄉 多 在 夢 中 遊 。

那 堪 更 聽 簷 前 雨 ， 點 點 聲 聲 滴 未 休 。

WRITING MY FEELINGS IN LATE AUTUMN

-Ching An (1851-1912 AD; the eight
fingered monk)

My body, alone as a cloud without a print.
This third time I come down south to listen to the
    temple's bell.
Each time I see wild geese that remind me of my home.
The mountains look sad in autumn,
yet a beautiful line rises from such sadness.
Old friends appear along my way.
Oh, when will I ever reach my goal of awareness!
I disappoint a thousand mountains.

暮 秋 書 懷

－ 敬 安 （八指頭陀，近代禪師）

身 作 孤 雲 無 定 蹤 ， 南 來 三 度 聽 霜 鐘 。

人 方 見 雁 思 鄉 信 ， 山 亦 悲 秋 帶 病 容 。

佳 句 每 淡 愁 裡 得 ， 故 人 多 在 客 中 逢 。

自 嗟 未 了 頭 陀 願 ， 辜 負 青 山 千 萬 重 。

AN OLD SAIL

-Chun An (Unknown monk, wose name
means 'a simple hut')

Then I lowered the sail,
and walked to shore.
Now I make sail,
in this tail wind.
If you would
sail with the wind,
why not wipe your feet
and climb aboard?

古　帆

- 淳　庵（僧，生平不詳）
（錄自禪宗雜毒海）

昔 年 到 岸 曾 收 卷 ，

今 日 因 風 又 展 開 。

若 要 隨 他 那 邊 去 ，

不 妨 洗 腳 上 船 來 。

Selected Sources

Cooper, Arthur, trans. *Li Po and Tu Fu.* N.Y.: Penguin Books, 1972.

Faccioli, Edoardo. *Chinese Calligraphy: From Pictorgraph to Ideogram.* New York: Abbeville Press, 1987.

Graham, A.C. trans. *Poems of the Late T'ang.* New York: Penguin Books, 1965.

Hamill, Sam, trans. *Facing the Snow: Visions of Tu Fu.* Fredonia, N.Y.: White Pine Press, 1988.

Herdan, Innes, trans. *300 T'ang Poems.* Taiwan: The Far East Book Co., 1973.

Kwok. C. H. and Vincent McHugh, trans. *Old Friend from Far Away: 150 Chinese Poems from the Great Dynasties.* San Francisco: North Point Press, 1980.

Red Pine, trans. *The Collected Songs of Cold Mountain.* Port Townsend, Washington; Copper Canyon Press, 1983.

Rexroth, Kenneth, trans. *One Hundred Poems from the Chinese.* N.Y.: New Directions, 1956; rev. 1971.

Rexroth, Kenneth, trans. *One Hundred More Poems from the Chinese.* N.Y.: New Directions, 1970.

Seaton, J.P. and Dennis Maloney, eds. *A Drifting Boat: Chinese Zen Poetry.* Fredonia, N.Y.: White Pine Press, 1994

Snyder, Gary, trans. *Riprap & Cold Mountain Poems.* San Francisco: Four Seasons Press, 1965.

Stryk, Lucien and Takashi Ikemoto, trans. *Zen Poems of China and Japan: The Crane's Bill.* New York: Grove Press, 1973.

Stryk, Lucien and Takashi Ikemoto, trans. *Zen Poetry: Let the Spring Breeze Enter.* New York: Grove Press, 1995.

Turner, John A., S.J. trans. *A Golden Treasury of Chinese Poetry: 121 Classical Poems.* Hong Kong: A Renditions Book, 1976.

Watson, Burton, trans. *Cold Mountain: 100 Poems by the T'ang Poet Han-shan.* New York: Columbia University Press, 1961; reissued 1970.

Wu-chi, Liu. *An Introduction to Chinese Literature.* Bloomington, Indiana: Indiana University Press, 1961.

Wu, John C. H. *The Golden Age of Zen.* Republic of China: United Publishing Center, 1975.